KAENJU

ESSAYS

AFTER BEING DIAGNOSED WITH STAGE 4 BREAST CANCER

Fujie Fukuda

福田富士技

CITI OF
BOOKS

CITIOFBOOKS, INC.
3736 Eubank NE Suite A1
Albuquerque, NM 87111-3579
www.citiofbooks.com
Hotline: 1 (877) 389-2759
Fax: 1 (505) 930-7244

Ordering Information:

Quantity sales. Special discounts are available on quantity purchases by corporations, associations, and others. For details, contact the publisher at the address above.

Printed in the United States of America.

ISBN-13:   Softcover   979-8-89391-324-8

             eBook   979-8-89391-325-5

Library of Congress Control Number: 2024919046

Table of Contents

Forward.. I

Chapter 1 : Diagnosed with Late Stage of Breast Cancer 1

Chapter 2 : My Daily Life 17

Chapter 3 : Countdown to my Final Day...59

Chapter 4 : And Today in 2024...77

Acknowledgments 81

Afterword..82

About the Author..84

A KAENJU Tree on My Home's Street

What is KAENJU?

Since 1988, I have been residing in South Florida, a region characterized by its subtropical climate. The plants and flowers here thrive in two distinct seasons: the dry season and the rainy season. One of the most striking trees in this environment is the Flame Tree, known as "KAENJU" in Japanese.

The Flame Tree, or Royal Poinciana, captivated me when I first arrived in this area. Its large, vibrant crimson flowers thrive under the intense sunlight, symbolizing the tropics' unique and vibrant spirit. The contrast of the crimson blossoms and green leaves against the blue sky creates a stunning visual that epitomizes the hot, lush environment of this region.

Forward

In this book, I share my thoughts and feelings shaped by life in the tropics, inspired by the beauty and resilience of the Flame Tree, "KAENJU."

Three years ago, I published "The Shadow of Coconuts," an essay that marked the beginning of a significant period in my life. Since then, many things have happened.

In May 2016, I was diagnosed with a recurrence and terminal stage of breast cancer. From that point, my focus shifted to planning how to live the short life ahead of me.

I noticed a new life at the end of the tunnel, one that opened up both my body and mind.

Living a meaningful life with limited time became a major issue for me. I documented my experiences and thoughts at each stage in daily journals, which became the foundation for this book.

Although my physical strength has declined, typing my feelings on a tablet has allowed me to spend a short period of quality life during these difficult times.

I would like to add that during this time, my cat, who lives with me, has been a great source of comfort and has played an important role in recording the happiness found in this book.

September 2018

Photo by: J. Grossman

Sunrise at Florida Beach

Chapter 1   Diagnosed with Late Stage of Breast Cancer

The Day Changed my Future Life Drastically

The underwent a seismic shift one sweltering May Day in 2008, when the typical Florida heat hung heavy in the air.

It was a day earmarked for my routine medical check-up, a choreographed dance of X-ray tests and sonograms that had become all too familiar.

Little did I anticipate the weight of the news that awaited me—a harsh reality delivered in the form of a diagnosis: stage 4 breast cancer. Despite my seasoned experience with the results of mammograms, where the majority had yielded benign findings, there lingered the memory of a cancer-suspect cyst from a decade prior.

However, this time around in 2016, the verdict was unequivocally grave, casting a shadow of uncertainty over my existence.

With surgical intervention looming on the horizon, I found myself navigating a labyrinth of emotions and decisions.

During my consultation with the surgeon, amidst the sterile confines of the medical office, I made a resolute plea—to have both of my breasts removed.

It was a decision borne out of years of grappling with the tumultuous landscape of breast-related health issues, an unyielding resolve that enough was enough. The doctor, attuned to the gravity of my request and the fortitude behind it, acceded with careful consideration.

As an elderly woman confronting the specter of mortality, I found myself at a crossroads, grappling with the notion of reclaiming agency over my own narrative. No longer willing to be tethered to the whims of fate, I resolved to seize control of my destiny, to rewrite the script of my existence in defiance of the disease that threatened to define it.

With the weight of reality settling upon my shoulders, I couldn't help but ponder the daunting question that loomed before me—what lies ahead for a cancer patient like me?

It was a question steeped in uncertainty, yet tinged with a glimmer of hope, a beacon guiding me through the murky waters of an uncertain future.

Human is Basically Lonely Being

In the whirlwind of appointments with doctors, enduring a barrage of tests, and navigating through various therapies to combat my cancer, each day seems to blend into the next. Despite the weight of my medical journey, the mundane tasks of daily life still beckon—reminding me of my solitary existence as I battle this relentless disease. It's as if living alone has become an inevitable part of my destiny.

Yet, amidst the chaos of appointments and household chores, I occasionally steal moments to pause and find solace. One such moment finds me seated on my favorite spot on the sofa, enveloped in the serenity of my living room, casting a contemplative gaze upon the tranquil haven of my backyard garden. As I draw in a deep breath and allow my eyelids to flutter closed, a profound question flutters through my mind like a gentle breeze:

"What truly defines the essence of human life?"

In that fleeting instant of introspection, a fleeting pang of loneliness dances across my consciousness, only to dissipate into the ether as quickly as it emerged.

In the midst of my personal musings, my attention is drawn to the delicate splendor of the pink and white blooms adorning my garden—a testament to nature's resilience and beauty. Yet, despite their captivating allure, society deems them as mere weeds, unwelcome intruders in the meticulously manicured landscape of human habitation. Their silent resilience in the face of adversity serves as a poignant reminder of the dichotomy between societal expectations and the innate beauty of the natural world.

Loneliness—a concept that had long eluded my thoughts since my migration from the bustling streets of Japan to the vibrant tapestry of American life.

For over five decades, my days were filled with the intoxicating allure of exploring new cultures, embracing novel experiences, and weathering the storms of life with unwavering resolve. However, as the specter of illness casts its shadow over my remaining days, the once-distant specter of loneliness now looms ominously on the horizon—an undeniable companion in my journey towards an uncertain future.

Tear in My Dried Eyes

The tests results of X-rays made clearly the truth that I had the cancerous tumor on right side of breast. Then the treatment would be starting very soon.

When I got home from Doctor's consultation of my breast cancer, first of all I phoned to my close friend about today's conversation with an oncologist.

She might be expected some kind of feeling about this report, or my voice from on the other side must be vulnerable for her.

So calmly encouraged me, my voice from on the other side must be vulnerable for her.

"I will help you with anything you need, so don't be alone, this is the meaning of friendship"

When I heard her kind words from the bottom of heart, I noticed my eyes were with full of tear.

What is this tear in my eye?

Her kind voice touched my heartstrings of me!

Even though in my long life past I have had numerals difficult incidents, my independent personality (strong personality) had avoided to showing these vulnerable feeling on my face.

Hormonal Therapy Sessions #1

I embarked on a new chapter in my battle against breast cancer with the start of a new drug therapy. Despite the explanations from the oncologist's assistant about what to expect, I couldn't shake the feeling of anxiety that gripped me as the day approached.

The treatment involved the injection of 500mg of the drug into my body, and while I tried to remain calm, the unfamiliarity of the experience only heightened my apprehension. Guided to a private examination room, I prepared myself for the procedure, feeling a sense of vulnerability as I exposed my buttocks for the nurse's administration of the injections. At the age of 80, any embarrassment I might have felt paled in comparison to the importance of the treatment.

As the nurse warned me that there might be some discomfort, the injection began. Each dose, injected slowly into the thick muscles of my buttocks, felt like an eternity, despite only taking about ten seconds each. But with each injection completed, I breathed a sigh of relief, grateful to have taken this step towards my recovery.

Returning home, I braced myself for any potential side effects that might arise from the treatment. Surprisingly, the first day passed without incident, and I felt a sense of relief wash over me. The first session of chemotherapy had been successfully completed, marking the beginning of a journey that would span ten sessions over the coming weeks.

With each session, I knew there would be challenges to face, but I also found strength in the knowledge that I was taking proactive steps towards my health and well-being. As I prepared for the next session, I carried with me the hope and determination to overcome whatever obstacles lay ahead on this path towards healing.

The Result of After 3 Months Therapy

It has been busy months after diagnosed breast cancer stage 4.

The life was changed to the abnormal from normal routine days.

Since I had retired, I has been at home most of time with my cat. However, many days a week when left house. I told my kitty every time "Be a good boy, taking care of home" and petting his head. Continuing this kind routine, a kitty knows when I dressed on going outfitted, it went to under the dining table.

The first of therapy was treated a radiation therapy per once a day. It's A set of 10 times. This is nothing heavy therapy at all. It was exposed on the spot of body for a several minutes.

When I had a first consultation, I request that I would not take so called a cancer chemotherapy at all. I knew how bad the side effect of chemotherapy was. It was a just general knowledge about the Chemotherapy, but I understand the side effects were terrible vomiting, headache, loosing hair, etc. this kind of side effects made me scared to take the treatment.

Over after a set of 10 sessions, relatively easy radiation therapy was what is the result?

After several weeks later, this initial cycle of therapy result was a positive to me. The oncologist told me that after examined by PET scan, was a positive which was cancer cells were not invade on my bone.

I felt I got one big step on my long journey of therapy ahead.

Without suffering of side effects so far, I am living a normal way.

I am appreciated a daily life more, even though I am having unfortunate illness.

Cleaning Closets in My House

As I embarked on the daunting task of cleaning out the closets in my home, a surge of determination coursed through me. Despite grappling with the relentless presence of cancer, I found a reservoir of energy within me, propelling me forward in my quest to declutter and organize.

As I flung open the doors of the closets, I was met with a dizzying array of items—remnants of a life lived over the span of five decades in America. Amidst the clutter, I couldn't help but recognize the weight of these possessions, once treasured mementos that now threatened to become burdensome relics of a bygone era.

Among the sea of belongings, there were treasures that held a special place in my heart—countless photographs capturing cherished moments, tokens of love and affection from family and friends, and a collection of beloved books that had accompanied me on my journey through life.

Yet, as I sifted through these precious artifacts, a bittersweet realization dawned upon me. While they held immense sentimental value to me, they would inevitably lose their significance in the wake of my eventual passing.

In the face of mortality, the ephemeral nature of these possessions became starkly apparent, prompting a pang of reluctance at the prospect of bidding them farewell.

Summoning a sense of resolve, I made a concerted effort to detach myself from the sentimental attachments that bound me to the past.

With each photograph and letter that I tenderly examined for one final time, I grappled with the conflicting emotions that swirled within me—nostalgia mingled with acceptance, sorrow tempered by a sense of liberation.

Slowly but surely, I relinquished my grasp on the tangible remnants of my past, bidding them a poignant farewell as I consigned them to the depths of a waste basket. It was a process that unfolded over the course of a week, each discarded memory serving as a poignant reminder of a life well-lived.

In the quiet solitude of my home, amidst the echoes of bygone memories, I found solace in the act of letting go.

For in bidding adieu to the physical manifestations of my past, I discovered a newfound sense of clarity and renewal—a testament to the transformative power of embracing impermanence and embracing the journey that lies ahead.

Peaceful Moments while I am Painting a Hibiscus Flower

My daily life has been filled with a series of doctor visits, week after week. These routines will likely continue for a while until a doctor finds a good prognosis for my condition. It may even go on forever.

When I feel a bit better, I seek solace in painting on canvas. This is the time I can forget about my illness and lose myself in the creation of art.

A few months ago, I discarded many things to simplify my life, but I still have a lot of art supplies at home. To save on expensive materials, I often paint new images over old ones. This time, I decided to create a new image of bright hibiscus flowers. Using the natural depiction of crimson hibiscus flowers helps to brighten my mood. My living room transforms into an art studio, with art supplies scattered everywhere.

My kitty sits on the sofa, seemingly evaluating the progress of my work.

Hibiscus flowers bloom all year round in Florida, though each individual flower only lasts a few days. This characteristic makes the hibiscus a perfect subject for my painting, bringing a lasting brightness to my living room decor.

Even though there is no deadline for finishing the painting, I know I need to consider it "complete" at some point. When I finally put down my brushes and sign my name, a sense of reality returns.

I wonder how the inside of my body is faring. It's now the second month of my medication therapy, and I'm nearing the end of the first scheduled treatment cycle. Even though the side effects are minor, I still worry.

The end of the therapy is still far off, and it will continue into the next month. A dark cloud starts to hover over my mind again.

Searching the Right Medication

More than 70 years ago, in my youth, I held a firm belief that relying on medications should be avoided whenever possible. Growing up in Japan, I embraced the notion that the body has a natural ability to heal itself, and I adhered to this philosophy for many years.

However, as I've aged and my physical strength has waned, I've come to realize the importance of modern medicines in supporting my health.

A few years ago, I received the devastating diagnosis of terminal breast cancer, and my oncologist stressed the vital role that medication would play in extending my lifespan.

I embarked on a journey of treatment, starting with a drug called "Ibrance" in 2016. Despite taking it for nearly two years, the results were not as promising as hoped. Subsequent medications, such as "Afinitor," were accompanied by intense therapies and injections, but the side effects became increasingly unbearable over time.

Severe itching plagued me day and night, leading to consultations with specialists and additional medications to manage the discomfort. Eventually, my oncologist made the difficult decision to discontinue "Afinitor."

In June 2020, I began a new medication called Vitrakvi by Bayer, which has proven to be a miraculous breakthrough. Despite the numerous potential side effects listed on the drug information, I have experienced none over the past four years. Thanks to this miracle medication, I am able to live a normal life and even continue working on my new book, KAENJU.

During the darkest moments of my treatment journey, I reluctantly turned to sleep aids to cope with the physical and psychological toll of my condition.

While they provided some relief, the next day often brought its own challenges, as the lingering effects of the medication left me feeling disoriented and unable to carry out my usual activities.

Despite these challenges, I am grateful for the advancements in modern medicine that have allowed me to continue fighting for my health and pursue my passions. Each day is a reminder of the resilience of the human spirit and the hope that springs from medical breakthroughs like Vitrakvi.

フロリダの空

(POEM) by Fujie Fukuda

空は微笑む ………．．

空は哀しむ………．．

空は泣く…………．．

時には大粒の涙を落とす、、、が、、、喜びも与えてくれるフロ
リダの空

朝明けの雲間からさす太陽の光は

私に生きる力を与えてくれる

青空に浮かぶ白い雲の群れ、まるで平原に散らばる羊のよう

足早く走る流れ雲，まるで海原で泳ぐ魚群のよう

膨らむ入道雲、愛した人の笑顔に変わり

私を見つめる

真っ赤に焼けた西の空，火炎樹の花の色

一輪私にささげて、暗い地の下に沈んで行く

ほのぼのと余韻を残して去った

美しいドラマ！

それはフロリダの空

Chapter 2   My Daily Life

A Joy of Having Pets

It's been heartening to see the warm and interested responses from my social network regarding my recent diary entry, "A Lovely Event," where I shared my deep affection for my beloved cat, Kelly.

For those who aren't particularly fond of pets, I hope my story provided a glimpse into the profound bond and mutual support that can exist between animals and humans.

Before Kelly came into my life, I didn't pay much attention to cats or dogs. However, as I faced the reality of living alone in my later years, I knew that a human companion wouldn't be a feasible option for the long term. That's when I made the decision to adopt Kelly eight years ago.

Since then, the impact of having Kelly by my side has been immeasurable. From the small, everyday moments to the significant milestones, Kelly has been a constant source of love and companionship, filling my life with joy and purpose.

I believe that my decision to welcome Kelly into my home has been mutually beneficial. He went from waiting in a small cage to living a happy life in our new home, and I gained a loyal and loving companion.

As I continue to share our daily adventures, I'm certain that our bond will only grow stronger, creating cherished memories that I'll treasure for years to come. Kelly's presence in my life serves as a reminder of the profound impact that pets can have, offering companionship, comfort, and unwavering love.

The story I once heard about the wealthy elderly person leaving a significant inheritance to his puppy resonates deeply with me now. It underscores the incredible bond that forms between humans and their pets, and the immense value they bring to our lives.

How lucky the dog was! I envy the incident.

Is my cat as much as lucky like the story?

I said "Yes".

In coming several episodes, I am going to talk about my cat, Kelly.

A Lovely Cat's Behavior

Besides of talking on the phone, my conversation is trivial one-sided conversations with my cat (Kelly, male cat) all day long.

Kelly is most of times by my side when I'm working on my PC, watching TV, or sometimes taking a nap in bed.

When he approaches me to tell his empty stomach for moving his mouth.

"It's too early for lunch, isn't it? wait" He understands the word "lunch, wait", and waits at sitting near me quietly.

If his lunchtime, (about noon) passed, then he makes a gesture "as if saying the lunchtime passed, I am hungry!" with moving his mouth.

One afternoon, as usual, I talked (it could be murmuring) to him looking at his eyes

"Kelly, you're a good boy. You slept in grandma's bed last night, so tonight you're going to sleep in your own bed" (a basket in the bathroom with a towel laid out so he can sleep.)

He looked at my face, I am not sure if he understood or not

In the early evening, I noticed he was not near me.

I was wondering where he was?

I looked for the places where he stayed on usual spots in house.

Then I found him curling in the basket at bathroom.

"Oh, what a good boy!"

I petted on his head, and at the same time I felt unexpected Kelly's behavior from what I said several hours ago to him, and at the same time my eyes welled up with happy tears.

It was as if he was asking, "Since you've told me to stay in my bed, so can I sleep on your bed tonight...?"

That night Kelly slept on my bed with me.

Kelly's Monologue

My Mom (a woman who adopted me) says, "Good night! Be a good boy and sleep quietly, I'll give you a delicious food tomorrow..."

Every night, my Mom tells me the same phrases and closes the door between her and me with a slam "ピッシャ".

Then, I stay in my bed room, which is mom's master's bathroom, with solitary for more than 7 hours until next morning around 7 am, when Mom gets up.

A dim light of the small digital clock makes the silhouettes in the room stand out. My pupils dilate widely and as a nocturnal person, this level of darkness doesn't bother me at all.My room is quite roomy, there are plates full with food, and water in a cup all the time. The litter box and 2 different types of sleeping beds are in my room.

I spend 7 hours, sometimes 9 hours, in my little studio apartment. I can run around the room and climb up and down the counter. If I make some noise, I hear "Kelly! quiet!" from the other side of the door.

I sit down quietly and dream of a delicious breakfast in the next morning.

One bed is a basket with a towel laid on it, another bed is a pet carrier covered with a towel for a hiding place from others.

The beds are very comfortable but I need to stretch sometimes, then I get out of the basket and lie down on small floor mat.

I do not like an air conditioner's drift so I go into one of the beds covered with a towel to make me warm and dark.

This pet carrier was used when I came to this house 7 years ago. Since I am grown up it is rather small for me, but I liked to crawl and curl up in a small space.

One day Mom bought me the nice bed with a roof, 4-5 years ago, but I have never used it. I do not like it. Mom encouraged me to go in the new bed, put my favorite snacks in the new bed, but I only eat the snacks and come out. That's it!

I can't explain why I do not like the nice commercial bed. It's still a mystery today

My room has no windows, so I don't know if it's bright or dark outside.

At 7 a.m., even though I can't read the clock in the bathroom, my physical clock tells me, "It's time to get up."

I hit the doorstop, bang! bang! to wake up Mom.

Some nights when Mom has taken sleeping pills, she'll probably still be asleep at 7am. When she wakes up by a single bang on the doorstop knob, she opens the door and looks like a sleepwalker. Then, she goes back her bed without saying a word.

Meanwhile I spend about an hour walking around the house, corner to corner, checking if everything is in order.

There's nothing unusual, just everything's OK. I jump up on her bed I lay down at Mom's feet and wait quietly for her to get up.

You probably notice that I'm a good boy, now.

If an hour passes and she still didn't wake up, I jump up and down on her bed and stomp on her legs and wake her up...

Then it's time for the long-awaited "a delicious breakfast!".

I watch and follow Mom's every movement, she opens the blinds and goes into kitchen. When she finally takes out my "delicious food" from the fridge, it's the greatest joy of the day.

You might be wondering what that "delicious food" is?

It's Hills science dry food. It was recommended by the store manager where I was before coming to this home.

My snack is the canned salmon.

It's selected from dozens of varieties, I get half a tablespoon of the same thing for my snacks.

Once before, she gave me a heaping spoonful as a reward for being a good boy, but that day I spat it out.

Since then, the amount of food and snack have always been the same, not too much, not small and this way keeps me in great shape.

My poop is also regular and great. I couldn't be healthier. Blessed on mom and me. At this time of year, during the winter in Florida, the sun shines in through the glass door at the entrance to the house.

The temperature in the room is 25-26 degrees Celsius, but it's cold for me walking around in the house with bare feet.

I find a sunny spot, the best seat in the house, and warm my whole body with my back to the sun.

My belly is full, the temperature is perfect, and I couldn't be happier than this environment.

To express my happiness, I say "meow" to my mom when she comes near me.

When the TV or music is on, I hide in refuge places. I really don't like these noises.

It's a strange but when mom uses the vacuum cleaner in the house, I watch the loud noise movement at a short distant from the machine.

If you ask me what's so interesting about their movements, my answer is I don't know. Sometimes she throws toys to me and plays with me, but I am not always in the mood, sorry mom! Generally speaking, cats eat, sleep, groom themselves, and then take naps most of times, that's the daily schedule for a house cat. That's true, I am an ordinary cat.

My Kitty's Episode

Winter in South Florida is the best season, with temperatures around 20°C at night and 27°C during the day. I couldn't ask for anything more. I'm just grateful and happy to live here.

As an elderly person, I don't have many exciting events happening every day to write in my diary. I simply wish for a peaceful and safe life each day, and I'm content with that.

In this uneventful daily life, my beloved cat Kelly has drawn my attention.

Except when he's hungry or wants me to play with him, his daily routine is to doze off near the glass doors, looking at the outside world. He is curious about the birds in the backyard and hopes small lizards will approach the other side of the doors.

One day, a tropical lizard entered the room through a gap in the door. Kelly caught it immediately. His catching ability was very sharp, not deteriorated at all despite being an old house cat.

He picked it up with his mouth and brought it to his room (which is also my bathroom), where he usually played with it by letting it go and catching it again.

This time, the lizard was about 4-5 inches long, quite big compared to the usual 2-inch lizards he catches.

I left Kelly in the room for a while to let him play with the lizard. After about 20 minutes, I came back to the room, but the lizard was gone. I looked for it, thinking it might be hiding somewhere, but I couldn't find it. Kelly seemed to have given up playing.

The next day, Kelly's appetite suddenly changed; he started eating more food and became more energetic. He usually ate 3-4 pieces of dry food at a time, eating several times a day.

This time, he ate his breakfast, lunch, and dinner all at once, emptying his plate every time. I was worried that something had changed in Kelly's health at the age of 9, but after a few days, he went back to his usual eating habits.

I wondered what caused his temporary behavior change.

Yes! That's right!

He might have eaten the lizard the day before!

I was relieved that he didn't vomit or have diarrhea after consuming a wild lizard. Even though he was a house cat that had never hunted for food, his instinct proved to be very active and well.

New Year's Day Mishap

めでたさも 中ぐらいなり 我が春 by 小林 一茶 (1763-1827)

"My New Year's Day is a half merry by Kitty's mishap" — Inspired by the haiku by Fujie's Witty Haiku

Today marks the first day of the year. The weather in South Florida is perfect—neither too hot nor too cold, with a few white clouds drifting across a blue winter sky. Kelly, my cat, seemed to be in a particularly good mood, running around the house from time to time.

I recalled an article I once read about cats, which mentioned that a cat might run erratically when it's not feeling well. Soon after, I discovered that Kelly had spat out some food on the carpet in my bedroom. The mess blended almost perfectly with the carpet, and I narrowly avoided stepping on it.

I found Kelly curled up, hiding in his cage. Instead of scolding him, I gently asked, "Aren't you feeling well?" and reassured him with a soft, "You're a good boy." As I cleaned the carpet, Kelly came over, as if to guide me to another hidden spot. "Here too," he seemed to say.

His behavior was so endearing that my unwanted task turned into a moment that made me smile.

Kelly had been eating the same crunchy snacks for seven years without ever growing bored, and he's always been in good health. But I had decided to be kind and give him something different this time, which seems to have backfired.

Unlike the traditional busy New Year's preparations in Japan—cooking festive dishes like o-zoni (お雑煮) and osechi ryouri (お節料理) or writing New Year's cards—this year was calm. No such tasks awaited me, but Kelly's little mishap was enough to make my New Year's Day feel half merry.

I Got a "Cat Punch!"

I was not busy from daily chores today, so I decided to treat something special for Kelly. When he finished his breakfast, I gave him dry bath and brushing, cleaning his eyes/ears. These things are my routine for him every day. Then, all the sudden, he gave me a "cat punch" on my both hands. (A cat punch is a gesture similar to human boxing. And its punching power is incredible.)

I wonder if I was being too lenient?

I was lucky not scratch me, and no bleeding this time. About 6 months ago, he punched me and I was bleeding. At that time, I reflexively hit him back on his nose. But this time I didn't scold him.

He might be warning to me that "Stop making noise! Leave me alone!" Usually, he is purring happily because he enjoys my actions.

Now I wanted to know about these cat's behaviors. I searched the internet, then I found it!

Cats do the punching when:

* When they're in a fighting mood

* When they feel scared

* When they're being touched repeatedly

* etc.

It found the reasons because I was too persistent to touched him. It seemed I exceeded the cat's "time limit" for doing good things.

Cats are very independent and don't obey their owners, as a dog owner knows already.

I learned recently from understanding between human relationship is not easy. Even with different species, cats and dogs to understand each other is more difficult. A human has to learn how to treat them and living both of us with peaceful relationships.

The end of cat's stories

My Taste Buds Changed Drastically

The end of World War II in 1945 marked the beginning of a period of significant change and evolution in the world. As someone who has lived through many of these transformations, I've witnessed firsthand the shifts in global environments and societal norms. But amidst these broader changes, I've also noticed shifts in my own personal tastes and preferences.

Growing up in a farming village on the western islands of Japan, potatoes were a staple part of our diet during the war years.

Alongside barley rice and vegetables from our small field, potatoes formed the backbone of our meals, providing sustenance during times of scarcity.

While other children in cities may have experienced hunger and deprivation, I was fortunate to always have something to eat, even if it was just potatoes prepared in various ways to fill our stomachs.

As our food situation gradually improved in the years following the war, I began to distance myself from the distinct smell and taste of potatoes that had once been so familiar.

For over three decades, I avoided potatoes entirely, steering clear of potato chips, french fries, and any dish that featured potatoes as an ingredient.

However, my perspective on potatoes began to shift after moving to America. With access to a diverse array of cuisines from around the world, my palate expanded, and I found myself craving new flavors and experiences.

Recently, I've found myself drawn back to potatoes, appreciating their versatility and subtle nuances in a way that I never did before.

It's a curious phenomenon, how our tastes and preferences can change over time, influenced by our experiences and surroundings.

In rediscovering my appreciation for potatoes, I'm reminded of the ever-evolving nature of our relationship with food and how even the most disliked ingredients can become beloved favorites given the right circumstances.

The Facts and Illusions

Lately, I've been noticing some changes in my vision. It seems like my eyesight is deteriorating, as I'm starting to see two moons in the night sky and struggling to read the subtitles on TV. Surprisingly, though, it hasn't really affected my day-to-day life.

Then, one day, I stumbled upon a shocking revelation. While peering into the bathroom mirror, I noticed something remarkable –

the wrinkles on my face seemed to be fading, and my skin appeared smoother and younger. Even the dark age spots under my eyes seemed to be disappearing. It was quite a pleasant surprise.

But here's the strange part – I realized that I hadn't changed my face cream or done anything different with my skincare routine. So, why was my reflection showing signs of youthfulness? It dawned on me that perhaps my vision was playing tricks on me.

You see, like most people, I don't wear my glasses or contact lenses when I'm washing my face or applying makeup. And without them, everything looks a bit softer and smoother. So, when I looked at my reflection without my glasses on, it seemed like I had magically turned back the clock on my appearance.

Feeling quite pleased with myself, I admired my seemingly younger reflection. But my satisfaction was short-lived. When I decided to take a closer look using a hand mirror with 3x magnification, I was confronted with the harsh reality – the image staring back at me was that of an aging old woman, far from the youthful visage I had imagined.

It was a stark reminder of the extent to which my eyesight had deteriorated. And yet, amidst this realization, I couldn't help but ponder the deeper meaning behind it all. While clear vision certainly brings a sense of peace and clarity to our lives, true happiness isn't always dependent on how we see the world. Sometimes, finding joy and contentment comes from within – from the fantasies and imaginings of our own minds.

I Saw the Gigantic Moon in the Sky

Songs about the moon have a timeless allure, with "Moon River" by Nat King Cole holding a special place in my heart as a beloved favorite from the early 1960s.

The moon itself has always held a fascination for me, especially when I recently beheld a stunning sight in the eastern sky—a large, orange moon illuminating the night. Later, a friend informed me that it was a thirteen-day-old full moon, adding a layer of mystique to the experience.

Through conversations with my friend, I delved into the art of predicting fortune and destiny based on the phases of the moon and other celestial factors. In Asian cultures, particularly in the historical Chinese calendar, the moon holds deep significance, with legends and sayings woven around its influence on human life.

In the evenings, I've observed fortunetellers stationed at street corners, offering insights into individuals' futures based on the alignment of the moon and other cosmic elements.

One evening, as I stepped into my backyard around 7 p.m., I was greeted by the sight of an unusually large, orange moon hanging low in the sky. It appeared almost surreal, resembling a colossal balloon suspended in the darkness above. I had to pinch myself to believe it was real. Returning indoors, I couldn't shake the image from my mind. Venturing outside once more, I was met with the same mesmerizing spectacle—a massive orb dominating the night sky with its radiant glow.

As the weeks passed, I encountered the full moon once again, its size mirroring that of the awe-inspiring sight I had witnessed before. It was then that I began to question my perception, realizing that my eyes may have been playing tricks on me, creating an illusion of a larger-than-life moon hovering in the heavens.

Though my initial excitement was tempered by this realization, the memory of that enchanting sight remains etched in my mind—a reminder of the beauty and wonder that the moon inspires, regardless of its size or appearance.

The Vocabulary I Learned After My Eyes Surgery

As an elderly person, it's common to face eye conditions like cataracts. When I noticed my vision deteriorating, I decided to undergo cataract surgery to replace the lenses in my eyes.

The surgeries were scheduled a week apart for each eye. Once the eye patches were removed, I was amazed at how clear my vision had become. It felt as though my youthful eyesight had returned. Although I've had multiple surgeries on my body in the past, this eye surgery was by far the most life-changing.

However, a day after the surgery, I noticed a small spot moving in my field of vision. Concerned, I asked my doctor about it. He explained that it was a common phenomenon called a "floater," and nothing to worry about.

Later, a Japanese friend told me that the floating spot is called "hi-fun" in Japanese, which translates to "flying mosquito" (飛蚊). Despite being 77 years old, I had never heard this term before. Learning how to write it in Japanese made perfect sense and I memorized the new vocabulary instantly.

Reflecting on this, I realized that if I had learned other things in my life as easily as I learned this word, I might have been a much smarter person today. However, my memory isn't what it used to be. Nowadays, I struggle to remember names. For example, someone will introduce themselves, and within seconds, I find myself asking, "What was your name again?"

It's frustrating that my brain seems to resist remembering names. Nonetheless, this experience reminded me that it's never too late to learn something new, and even small moments of learning can be quite satisfying.

The Orchids Flowers at my Backyard

Nature knows when it's time for flowers to open. My orchid plants have been sleeping for almost a year. The first flower opened this morning, which is lucky because it's February.

In February, most places in North America are in the middle of winter. But in Florida, February is the most pleasant season of the year, with temperatures around 80 degrees Fahrenheit during the day and comfortable nights between 60-75 degrees Fahrenheit.

In my small backyard garden, I have many orchids. Some are in pots, while most are on tree branches or hanging under the roof. A couple of times a year, when it gets cold at night, I bring the potted orchids inside.

This morning, I found three orchid flowers blossoming. They were pure white with thick, healthy petals. Orchid flowers have mysterious shapes, and paying attention to their formation can expand your imagination.

I've always been drawn to these flowers. I've painted them many times, but capturing their beauty, especially on white paper, is quite challenging. Once orchid flowers open, they last for several months. Sometimes, I get tired of watching them for so long, wishing they were like artificial flowers that stay beautiful forever.

When the time comes, a white withered flower drops from the stem, bidding goodbye. I've noticed that the first flower to open doesn't always drop first. The stronger flowers last longer, just like in human life.

It's the cycle of life, governed by nature's laws.

The Peak of Hurricane Season: A Personal Account of 2017

According to statistics, the peak of hurricane season occurs around September 10th each year. In 2017, this period proved to be particularly tumultuous, making it a model year for hurricane landfalls in Florida.

This year, hurricanes Harvey, Irma, and Jose followed one another in rapid succession, wreaking havoc across North America and causing billions of dollars in damages. As floodwaters from Harvey's devastation in Texas had not yet receded, Irma was already on its way, poised to strike the same regions again. The potential damage was incalculable.

Watching the destruction wrought by Irma on the Caribbean islands on TV was heartbreaking. I couldn't help but imagine my own home suffering similar devastation. However, the latest weather reports indicated that Irma's path had shifted slightly, providing a small measure of relief.

The Governor of Florida appeared on TV every few hours, urging residents in flooded areas to evacuate, saying, "We can restore your houses, but we can't save lives."

The Day of the Storm...

Fourteen hours later, at 2 PM, the storm raged on with alternating gusts of wind and rain. Fortunately, my house still had power, allowing me to watch continuous weather updates on TV, though I knew the power could go out at any moment. There was also a tornado warning for the area, heightening my anxiety.

Peering outside, I saw the fronds of palm trees in the garden swaying at right angles, testifying to the strength of the wind. The roar of the wind was incessant and unnerving. Irma was moving north along the east side of the Florida peninsula, and the sheer size of the hurricane, with a diameter of 400 miles, was terrifying.

The sound of the wind rang in my ears, adding to the tension. Even my cat, Kelly, seemed to sense the gravity of the situation, staying close and alert.

Living through 20 hours of relentless wind, rain, and gusts was incredibly stressful. Thankfully, there was no power outage in my area, so I could keep up with live coverage on TV. Every channel was dedicated to hurricane information and updates.

By evening, my internet connection was lost. How many more hours would this stressful, dark, and noisy ordeal last?

The Next Morning...

After a long and harrowing night, I looked out the window to survey the aftermath. Despite the terrifying winds, our garden had only

5-6 broken palm leaves scattered about. Venturing outside, I saw large branches lying on the road, blocking traffic.

Some neighbors were already out, beginning the cleanup process. Other than phone and internet outages, my house remained unscathed, a stroke of luck for which I was profoundly grateful.

As the storm moved away, calm and clarity returned. The sun was shining, and life seemed to breathe a little easier again. Kelly, sensing the tranquility, took a nap under the quiet afternoon sun.

The storm had passed, leaving behind a renewed appreciation for the calm that followed.

The End

Some Say It Was Better in the Past, But...

People often reminisce about "the good old days." Many who grew up after the war fondly remember a simpler time and say, "The old days were better!" I understand their sentiment. Today's lifestyle, dominated by smartphones, computers, televisions, and an array of automated devices, can feel overwhelming. Life moves so quickly that we often don't have time to pause and reflect, to find peace in stillness.

Yet, as much as we may miss the simplicity of the past, it is undeniable that we've become accustomed to the convenience and pace of modern life. It would be almost impossible to revert to the ways we lived 70 years ago.

But nature, in its raw power, often forces us to reconsider. The arrival of a super-powerful hurricane reminded me just how fragile modern life can be in the face of natural forces. In an instant, power was lost. Roads turned into rivers, homes were flooded waist-deep, large trees fell, and boats floated eerily down streets.

The devastation was staggering. When I saw the images of the worst-hit areas on television a few days later, it was even more horrifying than I had imagined. Power outages, disconnected phones, internet blackouts—it was as though nature had stripped away every layer of modern life.

In my area, we were fortunate. The damage was less severe. While we lost connection to the digital world for a few days—no phones, internet, or television—we were spared the destruction others faced. Even so, this temporary glimpse into life without modern conveniences served as a stark reminder of how much we rely on them.

For those few days, I felt as though I had stepped back into a different era, one where technology did not dictate every moment of life. It was humbling and oddly nostalgic.

The experience left me with a deeper appreciation for the tools and gadgets we often take for granted. While we may occasionally long for the simplicity of the past, there is also beauty and gratitude in the comforts of today. Even in their absence, these modern conveniences remind us to be thankful for the ways they enrich our lives—however fleeting their presence might be when nature decides to intervene.

Thunderstorms vs Firecrackers

July 4th is not only American Independence Day, but also the day I first set foot on American soil in 1970. Every year, Americans celebrate this national holiday with fireworks, but I'm not particularly fond of them. I still can't get used to the late-night fireworks that young people in the neighborhood set off, disturbing my sleep.

Since my cat Kelly started living with me, he's been terrified by the sound of fireworks every year, and I find it impossible to comfort him. I'm pretty fed up with the noise on this day and New Year's Eve. Even the faint sound of distant fireworks makes Kelly nervous. He has a phobia of the shooting sounds. As soon as he hears fireworks, he crouches under the table and won't come out. He instinctively knows that the dining table and its 20 sturdy legs provide a safe haven.

Speaking of phobias, people are afraid of many different things, such as spiders, Narrow spaces and heights often cause physical symptoms like a faster heartbeat. I am afraid of snakes and earthquakes. I can't explain why, but these fears are deeply ingrained.

Interestingly, the sound of thunder and lightning storms, which can be as loud as firecrackers, doesn't scare Kelly as much. Florida is known as the mecca of thunder and lightning. Despite living here for over 25 years, I still hate thunderstorms and can't get used to them. It might be an additional phobia of mine.

As Being a Voter of the Presidential Election of 2016

According to a poll, 46% of voters said they did not like either presidential candidate (as of September 2016).

I did not participate in that poll, but after watching the TV debates and gathering information from journalists, I found myself not liking either of the candidates—Donald Trump or Hillary Clinton—recommended by the Republican and Democratic parties. The voting day was about six weeks away, and I still couldn't decide what to do. I was simply observing the information. That was how I felt.

After the second debate between the two candidates, I realized my feelings hadn't changed much from a month ago. I hoped that maybe in the final debate, I would see who was best for the country and for me. But at this point, I wasn't sure which way to vote, and I felt like I might not choose either candidate, much like the 46% of voters in that poll.

The media also reflected the people's unstable mood. Despite the widespread dissatisfaction, it seemed this election was set to be more crowded than any in history.

I was disappointed by the previous eight years under the Obama administration. While the majority had chosen him, I felt many, including myself, were dissatisfied. Yet, as in any democratic society, we had to accept the decision and live with it. This time, regardless of who was elected—Clinton or Trump—I had little hope, but I knew we would have to follow the decision of the majority.

I had already cast my early vote.

Although political elections reflect the majority's will, I believe the changes in American politics will affect not only the U.S. but the rest of the world, as I have seen in the past. These changes will surely shape the lives of future generations, and while I hope there won't be drastic shifts during the remainder of my life, I feel that political, economic, environmental, racial, and international transformations are inevitable.

What kind of world will people born in 2016 experience when they grow up? All I can do is pray for their future. Good luck to the new generations!

Reflecting of Election Result in 2016

America is holding a presidential election with my personal hope so far.

Anyway, No more phone calls, no more texts on my PC!

Oh, I'm so happy!

At least my vote was useful.

The night of Election Day, the media was reporting that Ms. Clinton was in the lead by the polls, so I went to bed last night without watching the final result of the election.

Many people were swayed by Ms. Clinton, who was manipulated by some companies and celebrities and used a huge amount of election funds to get elected. Some TV stations were reporting as if she had already won.

This morning, I was just curious what the results would be, so I turned on the TV and was surprised to see the words "Donald Trump elected President."

I felt relieved and am happy that more than half of the American people made a good choice.

When I recalled how I had come to America, longing for the freedom and democratic society that has existed since the founding of the United States, it strengthened my belief in the responsibility of citizens to vote.

Every vote is important, and I voted early. That feeling paid off.

Watching the Inauguration of President Trump (January 2017)

The 45th new president of the United States has been born in 2017. Since Trump declared his candidacy over a year ago, I have been watching the presidential election with more interesting ever.

As an American citizen, I have been interested in the changes in political society and people's generations in recent years and have been watching curiously them especially.

I felt that America has changed in many ways from what I had imagined when I came to the United States 40 years ago. I think that this has been reflected in the inauguration of the new president.

In the past, I watched on TV about the presidential inauguration ceremonies since the time of President Reagan's election.

I have gradually come to understand the inauguration speeches clearly. I have been looking forward to the new presidential policies, but the great speeches also bring promise and hope, and as a result, it seems that the administration has always ended with not much change. I might be not clearly understand about politics well or that the way of the promises could not be complicated as he wanted.

This time, Trump's candidacy was a different one, as he was a businessman with no political experience, and just like many voters, I had doubts about him.

When Trump, who was elected by the Republican Party, began his election campaign on an equal footing with Clinton, who was supported by the Democratic Party.

I began to distrust the so-called "politician presidents" in the past and this time I eager to Mr. Trump will ministrants differently from the past presidents.

For the past eight years, the Obama administration has not been criticized in Japan and other countries, and it seems that it has been welcomed, but it seems that the results of the people's rebellion against the policies that left their own country, the United States, rather leading behind of other countries. That led to Trump's victory this time.

Trump made extremely unrealizable promises, but he raised the voice of the people and gained their approval.

When I think about whether the immature and unreasonable behavior of Democratic lawmakers, such as not attending the inauguration ceremony in January, will become common sense in modern political society, I wonder if it can be dismissed as the concerns of an old woman like me?

This might be my last participation of the presidential election. Therefore, I will be interested to see how it turns out.

As much as understanding, politics are so complicated and harder to complete own desire for complete the hopeful ministrations.

Glancing at Internet Information

There's an English proverb that goes, "Looking for a needle in a haystack." It means that finding something specific can be incredibly difficult and requires a lot of effort. We're all familiar with this challenge.

Today, however, we live in an information society where we can find answers to almost any question in just a few seconds by typing a keyword into a search engine of internet apps. I am very appreciative of living in this kind of convenient society.

Yet, in this age of information, searching for topics on the web often results in a massive amount of information. You must sift through it all to find the right answer. Additionally, you can find answers in various languages. Being bilingual, I benefit from this informational world. When I don't understand a word or expression, I can look it up in both English and Japanese. Such convenience was unimaginable when I was young, more than 50 years ago. Back then, I often skipped over questions I should have pursued.

Recently, I've been browsing blogs written by Japanese people and discovered that many Japanese have emigrated to foreign countries over the past generations, something I had never imagined. I wonder how many ordinary Japanese people know about this widespread emigration.

When I first came to this country, I thought living abroad was a great adventure, but it seems that in modern times, it's not considered a big deal anymore. The world today has changed at a tremendous speed, quite different from the progression of 100 years ago. Our world is now highly globalized, a change some citizens resist, but we must accept as a fact of life.

I often wonder what the world will look like 50 years from now. For people born and raised in the present era, they might not understand the feelings of us old-timers. Common sense and moral values will likely be different from ours, and they might not have a true sense of human connection as we do.

Standing on this transitional era, I have mixed feelings. In some ways, I feel sad. Human beings are the same as they were 100 years ago, but the people living in modern times are different from those who lived in the past. In terms of moral and spiritual aspects, such as kindness and value systems, modern people seem different from those who lived a century ago.

Convenience is Inconvenience

After my breakfast, I tried to log in my internet as a usual day activity. I noticed the red light flashing on the modem.

Oh no, there's another internet server problem!!

I had the problems of internet system several years ago.

I noticed a house phone was not working either. I got a double punch!!

In this way my troubled day was started.

Luckily this time, I could use my cell phone so I could contact to the server.

I was waiting for the repairman to come and would fix the problem possibly soon.

But……he worked hard an hour, he went back to his office. It seemed to be he had the unsolved problems by himself

I am not comfortable at home when someone stranger was around in my house.

The first day was over without fixing the problems.

On the second day, a new repairman who showed up around noon. He couldn't solve the problem also. He left my home without noticing to me. I was waiting a half day for the next service man came.

The third man finally arrived around 4 o'clock, almost the end of his working hours.

I started to getting irritated... I wondered how long it would be taken to fixe these modern technologies?

The modern technologies are very convenient but at the same time very inconvenient under the certain situations.

At 4:45 pm, my house phone rang after two days of silence and had having such an anxious time for a long hours and days.

"Hello"

I heard a voice from other end of line "the repair was completed"

The sound of the phone ringing this time was as gratitude as the time half a century ago when I was waiting for a phone call from my love.

Different Cultures

It's common knowledge that different places have different customs, but sometimes the differences can be surprising.

One of my friends recently returned from a vacation in Hawaii. I asked her, "How was your trip?" She excitedly recounted her first-ever experience with an earthquake, a 5.6 magnitude one that caused significant swaying, and how she toured the lava fields by helicopter, marveling at the natural wonders Hawaii has to offer.

Naturally, I was curious about the beaches, since she's very familiar with the long, wide beaches of Florida. Her answer was fascinating— she mentioned the unique black volcanic sand beaches of Hawaii. Although she was intrigued by the unusual black sand, she wasn't particularly impressed by the beaches themselves, noting they were small compared to the miles-long expanses of Florida's coastline, which she was used to walking.

What puzzled her most wasn't the beaches themselves, but the behavior of some beachgoers. She noticed a woman, who she guessed was an Asian tourist—likely Japanese—sitting on the beach with a pretty umbrella. The woman was completely covered in white clothing, including a hat and gloves, while sitting under the umbrella. This was strange to my friend, as beachgoers in Florida usually sunbathe in swimsuits or cover up lightly, but rarely like this.

She asked me why the woman was dressed that way on the beach. I explained that in many Asian cultures, especially in Japan, people are very concerned about UV protection and avoid tanning, considering pale skin to be a sign of beauty. It's common for people to cover themselves with layers of clothing, hats, and gloves to shield from the sun. However, even for me, having lived in the U.S. for years, it seemed unusual to sit on a sunny beach dressed that way.

This conversation reminded me of how cultures differ all around the world. When I first saw women in Middle Eastern countries wearing full black garments that covered their faces, I also found it surprising. I remember wondering how they managed to stay cool under all that clothing, especially in hot climates, and how they enjoyed the beach or swimming.

But my curiosity was rooted in a lack of understanding about the religious and cultural reasons behind their attire. For instance, in Islam, modesty is highly valued, and covering oneself is a way of expressing that modesty. Even though it may seem unusual from an outsider's perspective, for these women, it's a deeply ingrained and respected practice.

I think back to Japanese customs and how they may also appear odd to others. Before the COVID-19 pandemic, when I saw videos of people in Japan walking around town or shopping while wearing masks, I found it a little strange, despite understanding the reasons behind it. In Japan, wearing a mask is a common courtesy to avoid spreading or catching a cold, and also to protect against seasonal allergies.

In contrast, in the U.S., masks were traditionally only seen in hospitals or in highly contagious environments. If someone in America had a cold and was coughing, they would usually just cover their mouth with a hand or tissue.

These small cultural practices show how our behaviors are shaped by the environments, traditions, and beliefs we grow up with. What's normal in one part of the world can be seen as odd in another, and often, it's these differences that spark curiosity and lead to a deeper understanding of our shared humanity.

Living Under the Strict Society During the COVID-19 Pandemic

As a little girl during World War II (1941-45), I couldn't fully comprehend the fear and uncertainty gripping the world. Now, 75 years later, as I approach the end of my life, I never dreamed I would face another global crisis: the COVID-19 pandemic. Many people did not realize just how terrifying such a pandemic could be until it became a reality.

The constant media coverage of COVID-19 only heightens the fear and anxiety among citizens. Government authorities urge people to stay home as much as possible to avoid spreading the virus.

For me, staying home has been a part of my routine for many years, so I decided to use this time to delve into understanding government systems—something I had never paid much attention to before.

The internet has become an invaluable resource, providing easy access to information without the need to leave the house. This period of strict isolation has given me a chance to learn about the workings of government and politics, areas I had previously neglected.

When I was younger, living in Japan, I didn't take much interest in politics and often abstained from voting. Now, despite not having voting rights in Japan anymore, I find studying government systems enriching and insightful, regardless of the country.

This enforced isolation and the unfortunate situation brought on by the pandemic have, in a way, turned into an opportunity for me to gain a better understanding of the world. I hope that by learning more, I can pass on this knowledge to future generations.

Ultimately, even in times of crisis, there can be silver linings—opportunities to learn, grow, and better understand the world around us.

Looking Up the Bright Side of the World

A woman (me) wakes up from an afternoon nap, a familiar part of her daily routine. She finds herself in a daydream, gazing out into the sky.

Looking westward, she sees dark clouds gathering, signaling a heavy downpour in the distance. But then, turning to the eastern sky, a massive chunk of white cloud floats peacefully against a backdrop of deep blue.

Two contrasting skies—one promising rain, the other basking in serenity. It's as if two different worlds exist at once: one bright and hopeful, the other gloomy and uncertain.

This duality mirrors our human world today. The pandemic looms like the stormy sky, dividing us into two distinct realities. In one, people are engulfed in political and economic uncertainty, unsure of what comes next. Yet, in democratic countries, we at least have the choice, the freedom to determine our own future.

In contrast, those living under communist or dictatorial regimes lack such freedoms. They might not even realize what they're missing, not having experienced the possibility of choice.

The woman feels immense gratitude for living in a democratic society, where she has the right to hope and dream, despite the challenges of the present.

Even amid the global crisis of COVID-19, it's time to look up—toward hope and recovery. There will come a day when good news finally arrives to tell us, "The nightmare is over."

She is also thankful for the courage to face her own battle with a life-threatening illness, even while the world faces pandemic-induced despair. Despite everything, she sees a ray of light in the future of medicine, a beacon of hope for both herself and the world.

Unusual Accident

Accidents often strike when we least expect them, yet some mishaps are foreseeable with a bit of caution.

Tripping over objects or slipping and falling are common accidents that can often be avoided with careful attention. However, there are also unforeseeable events like car accidents or natural disasters such as earthquakes that are beyond our control and fall under the realm of fate.

Today, I experienced a rather comical yet avoidable accident.

I had ordered some rice cakes online and decided to bake them in the oven. After a few minutes, they puffed up beautifully, indicating they were ready to eat. Eager to indulge, I reached out to test their softness with my finger.

What happened next was entirely unexpected.

As I pressed my index finger against the rice cake, expecting a soft texture, I yelped in pain.

The thin outer layer of the mochi tore open, and my finger became ensnared in the piping-hot rice cake. In my reflexive attempt to pull away, the sticky mochi clung stubbornly to my finger, resulting in a quick but painful burn.

Despite the mishap, I couldn't resist sampling the baked mochi, dipping it in a traditional Japanese sauce made with yuzu miso and soy sauce.

To my delight, it was delicious, evoking fond memories of my childhood when my mother used to make similar treats.

As I nursed my blistered finger, I couldn't help but reflect on the nature of accidents in the kitchen. While burns from hot pots or cuts while chopping vegetables are common occurrences, burns from baked rice cakes are certainly a rarity.

As we age, our skin becomes more delicate, much like how our internal organs may not function as efficiently as they once did in our youth. In light of this, I'll need to keep a supply of bandages handy for the next couple of weeks as I wait for my finger to heal completely.

In the kitchen, as in life, accidents are an inevitable part of the journey. While some may leave us with a few scars and a cautionary tale to tell, others, like my encounter with the baked mochi, serve as a reminder to approach each mishap with humor and resilience.

Two Ways of "K" Cleaning (Kitty and Kitchen) in the House

There's an old saying: "Maggots thrive among widows", which has a modern echo in the belief that "Women living alone tend to get dusty". Perhaps it's a reflection of busy women today, pressed for time and struggling to find a moment for housework. I might be one of them.

For the past few years, I've been occupied with caring for a friend and self-publishing my book (in 2015), so cleaning the house has always been the last priority.

It's been a long time since I last cleaned under the electrical appliances on the kitchen counter. I moved into this house seven years ago, so maybe it's been that long...

Today, I finally decided to tackle it. Armed with a bleached dish towel, I carefully moved each item—a blender, kettle, microwave—and began wiping around them. Expecting to find a shockingly dirty surface, I was surprised when the white towel came back almost clean. Maybe I had cleaned it a few years ago, though my memory isn't as sharp as it once was.

In my world, wiping around the appliances and keeping the countertop neat is just another part of cooking.

Now, about the other "K"—the kitty. My biggest concern is the cat hair that sheds constantly. Unfortunately, when I adopted my cat, he wasn't trained to take baths. With his size (17 pounds!), I can't manage bathing him alone. Grooming services? Yes, but they're beyond my budget.

So, I groom him morning and night, brushing his fur, cleaning his eyes and ears, and giving him a "dry shower" by wiping him down with a wet towel. It's become a daily routine, and my cat, Kelly, loves it. He purrs with joy, especially when I give him a firm back massage.

"Come on, Kelly! Time for brushing..."

When I call him from across the room, he silently trots over and sits down, waiting. Isn't that adorable?

Grooming Kelly has become one of my happiest moments each day, a time of simple bonding between us.

As for the kitchen... well, I confess I slack off on that a bit more often.

Observation of Nature's Rules

It has now been 10 years since I moved into my current home—a place filled with hope and endless possibilities. Even in retirement, I felt a surge of excitement and energy, fueled by dreams of creating the perfect home and tending to a beautiful garden. This house, brand new when I moved in, has given me not only shelter but also a canvas to express my love for nature, especially in the small backyard where I began planting a variety of flowers.

In the early days, I relished every moment spent outdoors, working with the soil, and planting. But I soon learned that gardening in a semi-tropical climate like this is nothing like what I had experienced during my years living in the northern states of America. My knowledge of plants, carefully cultivated over the years, seemed inadequate here. It was almost as if the rules of nature had shifted, forcing me to adapt and learn anew what kinds of plants would thrive in this new environment.

My first big mistake was choosing plants like the white bird of paradise and dwarf banana plants—tropical beauties that thrive in zones 10-11. They looked so attractive in the beginning, full of promise with their exotic appearance, but they quickly grew out of control. Within two years, they became too large and unmanageable for me. The physical labor of tending to them was overwhelming, and I realized I couldn't handle it on my own. When I finally decided to remove them, I discovered yet another challenge: although cutting them down was easy enough, their roots continued to grow and regenerate. Within just six months, the plants were taller than me—over five feet high! It was then that I asked a young neighbor to help me dig out the roots, which he did using an axe. The sheer difficulty of removing those stubborn root systems was a reminder of how relentless nature can be.

This experience taught me to seek out plants that required less maintenance. I eventually found solace in tropical air plants and orchids, which seemed to be the perfect solution. They required virtually no care; I could simply place them on tree branches, and they would bloom effortlessly, season after season. It felt like a small victory—a peaceful coexistence with nature where I didn't have to fight or struggle to maintain control.

One orchid, in particular, had been a consistent joy for several years, blooming luxuriously with minimal effort on my part. However, this past season, something was different. Most of the buds fell before they could bloom, leaving me puzzled. Why was this happening? Could it be the plant's old age? Or perhaps it was simply tired of being in the same spot for too long? It was a mystery that I couldn't fully unravel, a reminder that even when we think we understand nature, there are always surprises.

In contrast, the white lilies I had brought with me from my previous home—a plant I received almost a decade ago—continued to flourish with an almost defiant strength. These lilies, much like invasive weeds, had survived every attempt I made to get rid of them. They were hardy and stubborn, growing vigorously no matter what. But despite their relentless nature, they gave me a gift every spring: during the

Easter season, they blossomed into beautiful white flowers, year after year. It was as if nature, despite its wild unpredictability, still found ways to bring me moments of grace and beauty.

As the years passed, my relationship with my garden began to change. Where I once found joy in the act of gardening itself, I now find myself more inclined to simply observe the subtle rhythms of nature. The excitement I once felt about planting and watching things grow has shifted into a quieter appreciation of the natural cycles unfolding before me. I recently moved a Phalaenopsis orchid from my living room to the garden. It had begun to lose its vitality, and when it dropped a flower, I knew it was time to let it live in a more natural environment. Interestingly, the flower that fell hadn't even opened fully before it dropped to the ground. This small, quiet moment reminded me of something profound—just like in human life, nature doesn't follow the expected order. The firstborn does not always die first, and life unfolds in ways that defy our attempts to control or predict it.

Being of Japanese ancestry, I often think about the Japanese tradition of cherry blossom viewing, a cultural event that has been cherished for generations. In Japan, people gather to admire the short-lived beauty of the cherry blossoms, knowing that they will last only a few days before falling. Depending on the weather—whether it's rainy or windy—the flowers might stay in full bloom for just a day or two. Yet, this brief moment is celebrated with great joy, and people look forward to it year after year, anticipating the return of that fleeting beauty.

But as we admire the blossoms, we often overlook nature's more hidden aspects. After the flowers fall, no one goes out to marvel at the decaying petals scattered across the roads and rivers. Perhaps only the cleaning crews witness this quieter, less glamorous side of nature. In my own garden, I've noticed a similar pattern. I have planted flowers that bloom at different times and for varying durations. Irises and hibiscus grace me with their beauty for just a day before they wilt. Lilies bloom for a few days, while orchids can last for months. Zinnias, resilient and hardy, bloom nearly all year round.

My computer is filled with photos of my garden, capturing the flowers at their peak—vibrant and full of life. Yet, interestingly, I've never taken a picture of them just before they wilt and fall. Perhaps it's because I hesitate to record the sadness that comes with their decline. It seems to be a natural human tendency to focus on beauty and avoid confronting the inevitability of decay.

Every time I see a withered flower in my garden, I am reminded of the words "the destiny of rising and falling in nature." Nature follows a cycle of growth, blooming, and fading away, and as humans, we are no different. We, too, are part of this natural world, subject to the same cycles of growth and decline. But when I look back on my life, I find that I don't want to focus on these inevitable declines. Why is that?

Perhaps, like the flowers in my garden, I prefer to remember the moments of my life when I was at my peak—those times of joy, vitality, and abundance—rather than the periods of loss and decline. It is a natural human emotion to hold on to the highlights, to treasure the memories of our best moments, and to let the less glamorous realities fade into the background. As I grow older, I find comfort in this perspective, just as I find comfort in the quiet beauty of my garden, where life blooms and fades in its own time.

A Peaceful Day

Our days are a continuous series of emotions from the moment we wake up until we go to sleep. I imagine this routine is familiar to most people. My day started with a gentle nudge from my cat at 5 a.m.

"Oh, so early!" I thought, still half-asleep.

I got up and opened the door to my kitty's bedroom (the master bathroom), turning on the light. To my surprise, Kitty was still curled up on his bed, gazing at me as if to say, "What's wrong? It's too early for you!" It was then I realized my mistake—I had misread the digital clock. I promptly returned to bed, waiting for the correct time to take my medication at 7:00 a.m.

One of the highlights of my cat's day is the morning meal of chicken-flavored dry food, which he eagerly looks forward to.

At 10:30 p.m., after completing his nightly routine of brushing, eye and ear cleaning, I gently pet his head and say, "I'll give you something tasty tomorrow. Good night." He then quietly settles down and waits patiently for the next morning, giving me a peaceful 7–8 hours of sleep.

Watching political and social news on TV often leaves me feeling pessimistic, a reminder of the realities of the world. Even so, my routine, simple and repetitive, offers me a sense of peace.

What about your routine? Does it bring you peace, or does the chaos of the world seep into your day?

Photos by: J. Grossman

Activities in the Early Morning at South Florida Beach

Chapter 3   Countdown to my Final Day

I Am Feeling Well Today

It's a Saturday after the holidays, and the sun has been shining brightly since the morning. My cat, Kelly, is stretched out in a sunspot inside the house, basking in the warmth with an air of pure contentment and happiness.

Today, for the first time in a while, I've been feeling well. I even had the energy to vacuum the house, a small but significant accomplishment. Afterward, I lay down on the sofa to catch my breath and stared out at the garden, where the sun gleamed brightly. The sky was a perfect, clear blue, without a single cloud in sight, framed by the swaying palm leaves.

I decided to open the door wide, letting fresh air into the house—a rare treat, given how often the weather is either too hot, rainy, or windy, or there's the noise of landscapers working nearby. But today, everything was just right. The temperature was a comfortable 23 degrees Celsius, neither hot nor cold.

With no pressing chores or obligations, I simply enjoyed the quietness of the day. Moments like this, where everything aligns so perfectly, are rare, and they bring a sense of peaceful happiness that's difficult to describe. It's a reminder that being alive, in itself, is a kind of happiness.

Everyone experiences happiness differently. Some find it in the hustle and bustle of a crowded mall, others in the satisfaction of a meal at a popular restaurant, or the thrill of connecting with nature on a mountain hike or at the beach. Each person's sense of happiness is unique, shaped by their own experiences and desires.

Today, my happiness came from something small and unusual—something that others might overlook or not understand. But for me, it was a moment of contentment in my own reality, living with and surviving breast cancer. This simple day was a reminder that happiness can be found in the quietest, most ordinary moments of life.

Revealing My Secret

The day August 1, 2017, a day I feel compelled to mark in writing.

The year, I turned 77, celebrating my birthday just two months ago. But I wonder if it's right to celebrate, given the strange occurrence that has been bothering me these past few weeks.

About two weeks ago, my favorite shopping bag—a bag that wasn't particularly valuable but one I liked a lot—vanished. I felt as if I had been tricked or cursed, and I've spent days feeling frustrated and uneasy about its sudden disappearance.

I assumed I had lost it when visiting a friend at a nursing home, perhaps even having it stolen. The bag was quite pretty, after all. I allowed myself to think it was someone else's fault, which is probably typical of elderly people like me. I blamed external forces, frustrated, even though it wasn't a high-priced item.

Ten days passed, and I had nearly given up on ever finding it. Then, today, I discovered it in the most unexpected place: under the kitchen sink!

I live alone, so there's no one else to blame for putting it there, no one to accuse of playing tricks on me. And it's certainly not a place where my cat would have hidden it. So, why did I put it there? I have no memory—none—of placing it under the sink.

This whole situation has left me uneasy. I've always acknowledged the physical deterioration that comes with age, but I've held strong in my belief that my mind, my brain, would stay sharp. But now? I'm not so sure. What happened this time seems unusual, even for someone who forgets things occasionally. My friends, many of them in their 60s, laugh about their own forgetfulness, reassuring me that it's normal. But... this feels different.

A part of me whispers that I need to be cautious. I'm undergoing chemotherapy for breast cancer, and the medications are strong. Maybe, just maybe, they're affecting more than just my physical body. Perhaps they're working their way into my mind, weakening my ability to trust my own memory.

And that thought—losing trust in my mind—is far more unsettling than any misplaced shopping bag.

Losing My Best Friend

It's been about half a century since I first met him.

My irreplaceable best friend, the person who shaped my life, passed away yesterday, Christmas morning.

My best friend, who was involved in countless moments of my life and helped me create many memories, was unable to go beyond 96 years old. Despite this, he had a happy and exciting long life and passed away peacefully in his eternal sleep.

He had been speechless for about a week, but his wife and friends were by his bedside, and they seemed to understand what we were saying to him.

I had always expressed my gratitude to him, even when he seemed to be in a coma before taking his final breath. My final words of farewell were short,

"Thank you very, very much!" I said in his ear.

When I touched his hands, they were still warm.

It was a sad moment, but at the same time, I felt a bit of relief to see him no longer struggling to survive after many months. Now he sleeps in peace forever.

The Avocado Tree

My backyard is very small, but it's just the right size for me to take care of by myself. I love gardening, pulling out weeds, and trimming the bushes. It's a manageable job, not only keeping my garden pretty but also providing reasonable exercise for an aging person like me.

I've planted tropical fruit trees such as citrus, avocado, and banana in my backyard. Avocado is one of my favorite fruits. After enjoying an avocado, I planted its seed in the corner of my garden, hoping that someday I could eat a fruit grown in my garden without any chemicals.

In Japan, it's said that "It takes three years for peaches and eight years for persimmons, chestnuts to grow for their harvest." I guessed that avocado would take just as long. I thought it would take at least five years to pick my own avocados from my garden.

In early spring 2017, I anticipated harvesting avocado fruits after planting the seed. I understand that plants in tropical regions grow very quickly and can become large trees. That's why my community has strict rules prohibiting certain trees from being planted near homes.

However, I planted the seed a year ago. It grew taller, and I trimmed it often to avoid drawing attention from my neighbors. Now it's grown to about my height. If I had let it grow freely, it would surely have become a 15-meter tree within several years.

One day, I looked up, thinking it was time to trim the tree again, but I found some flowers blooming at the ends of the new branches! So, I decided to stop trimming. It was exciting, and every time I stepped into the garden, I looked at the flowers.

About a month after I first saw flowers on the branches, I didn't see any fruits. With my poor eyesight, I couldn't see anything at all. Maybe this tree was male, so there were no female flowers.

A few days later, I found just one pea-sized avocado hanging on a branch. The small fruit was camouflaged by green leaves, which is why I couldn't see it earlier.

Recently, we haven't had much rainfall, so I water the tree every evening. Watering is one of my enjoyable activities. From sunrise to sunset, these kinds of daily routines bring me happiness and make my remaining days meaningful.

This month, my calendar has been filled with a string of appointments for physical exams, medical examinations, and follow-up examinations...

PS: Last year, I grew bananas. One bunch produced 50 bananas, which was too much work to maintain, so I cut them down.

Vanishing Without Fulfilling Its Own Life

In the summer of 2017, there was an incident that felt like a microcosm of the human condition.

A little over two months ago, I discovered an avocado bud at the end of a branch that I had grown from a seed I planted. Watching it bloom was a source of joy for me, and a few weeks later, I found a small fruit. It was not just a joy but an exciting incident.

How many weeks has it been since then? My joy continued as the pea-sized fruit grew large enough to be photographed without zooming in from under the tree.

I eagerly anticipated the day I could taste an avocado from my garden.

About three days ago, I went out to the garden to take another photo, but the fruit was gone. It couldn't have been taken by birds or squirrels because it was still hard-skinned and located at the tip of a small branch.

I wondered if it couldn't endure the harsh weather of over 30-degree hot days. Was it destined to be impossible to achieve a mature life?

Then, I found a tiny avocado lying near its parent tree trunk. It was still green, and it must have only recently fallen.

I said "goodbye" as it would now become a nutrient for the parent tree.

Here, I watched the "drama of nature's law" unfold.

Barometer of Happiness

If you are blessed with a good environment, financial stability, supportive relationships with family and friends, and decent health, you might be considered a very happy person by many. Such people are often envied, and it is generally believed that they live fulfilling lives.

However, I question whether having all these things truly defines happiness. It seems to me that real happiness comes from accepting and being satisfied with your life, regardless of circumstances.

When you're young, it's common to challenge your dissatisfaction and work hard to achieve your goals. This drive gives you a sense of purpose and satisfaction, which many equate with happiness. For the majority, this pursuit of goals and dreams brings a sense of fulfillment.

But as we age, our perspectives shift. I've been diagnosed with terminal breast cancer and my life has changed significantly. I now take more medications, visit the doctor more frequently, and have had to adjust my lifestyle. While these changes aren't things that make me particularly happy, they don't make me feel unhappy either.

I've come to accept my situation and find satisfaction in the life I've lived. It's not about being a "loser" in life but about finding peace with where I am now. Happiness, I've learned, isn't something that can be measured or compared with others. It's deeply personal and unique to each of us, shaped by our acceptance of ourselves and our circumstances.

Sentimental Moments

Aging often brings with it a profound sense of loneliness that is difficult to ignore.

While there are certainly positive aspects to this later phase of life—such as the freedom that comes from being free of job responsibilities and the demands of raising children—the reality is that life rarely unfolds exactly as we hope or expect. This unpredictability, in fact, may be one of the truest insights we gain about what it means to be alive.

Reaching old age can introduce challenges that affect not only one's own health but also the daily routines and lifestyle of a partner, if one is married. Additionally, shifts in our parents' health, if they are still alive, and various other aspects of life can gradually turn into sources of stress that are difficult to ignore or to manage.

Accepting these harsh realities as they come often requires time, patience, and an inner resolve.

In the event of a sudden misfortune, such as the loss of a loved one, the impact can be staggering and almost unimaginable. However, with time, the initial shock usually softens, and we eventually begin to find a way back to a sense of normalcy, even if life will never be quite the same.

So, how can we effectively handle these current challenges that sometimes feel unbearable? While I don't have a definitive answer from my own experience, I would say that perhaps the best approach is to "accept it as part of your fate" and continue moving forward.

For someone like me, who has been single my whole life, there are likely aspects of both the sorrow and the sweetness that I have not fully experienced or understood.

Each of us holds a unique answer to life's difficult questions, but no one can truly tell you what path is best for you as an individual.

A Life That Doesn't Go the Way You Want

Since I turned 60, I've often looked back on my life, wondering what kind of person I would become as I prepared for the end. Now, as that time seems to be approaching, I find myself treating cancer—a reality that is painful but, in some strange way, feels like the direction my life was always heading towards, even if I never consciously planned it.

Life, as we all know, doesn't always go the way we want. It unfolds in ways that are often beyond our control, guided by forces we can't fully understand. The truth is that no living thing can survive forever. Everything diminishes with time; it's the natural order of things. Some believe in reincarnation, the idea that life is a cycle and that we return to this world in another form. Whether or not this is true, there is something comforting in accepting the laws of nature and the inevitability of life's end.

As I glance toward the end of my life, I realize that, in some ways, I am living the life I subconsciously planned for myself years ago. I had always thought I would live to around 80 years, and now, even with the unpredictable reality of cancer, I find myself strangely at peace. It's as if

I've settled into a warm bath, comfortable in this life, with no desires or dreams pulling me toward something more.

I've learned that there is a certain peace in accepting the natural flow of life, in not struggling against it. Fighting against the inevitable only drains your energy and brings more unhappiness. Even now, with the pain and the struggle, I've found a way to coexist with it, to see it as part of the journey I've been on all along.

Ironically, as I face my own mortality, I have no complaints. I don't feel the need to chase after anything more. My life feels complete in a way, even though I'm not quite ready to leave it behind. I find myself speaking to God, asking Him to wait a little longer before welcoming me into His embrace. Yet, when I discovered my breast cancer had recurred, I found myself also asking Him to come closer, sensing that perhaps my time might come sooner than I once expected.

It's a strange place to be, caught between the desire to stay and the readiness to go. My feelings about death waver, especially when the pain and discomfort become too much to bear. But through it all, I am learning to find peace in the uncertainty, to let go of the life I once thought I could control, and to accept whatever comes next.

PS: My feelings about death shift in different directions, especially when the pain and struggles intensify. It's a constant balancing act between acceptance and resistance, between peace and the natural fear of the unknown.

What is a Human Life?

A human life begins with the cry of birth, as we emerge into this world and start the journey of growth and development. Over time, we mature, utilizing the functions and abilities that have been built up within us. As we move through the stages of life, we become fully realized human beings, capable of complex thought, emotion, and interaction—distinct from other animals.

But as we near the end of our lifespan, these functions begin to weaken. The vigor of youth fades, leaving us with only the basic functions that were present at birth. Eventually, these too cease, and we pass away.

The span of a human life varies greatly. Some are fortunate enough to live long, fulfilling lives, while others are cut short, sometimes tragically so. It's a stark reality that the average lifespan just 200 years ago was only around 40 years—half of what it is today. Yet, the length of life doesn't necessarily dictate its quality or significance.

Each human life is unique, shaped by experiences, relationships, and personal achievements. Reflecting on the lives of others, especially those close to us, offers a deeper understanding of our own mortality. I have witnessed this firsthand as I've seen many loved ones near the end of their lives.

My younger brother, confined to a hospital bed with an incurable disease, waiting for the inevitable. My biological mother, watching over him, knowing that she could do nothing to change his fate. An older sister, battling cancer with every ounce of strength she had, only to eventually succumb after enduring the loss of two of her own children.

These experiences have forced me to confront the reality of death repeatedly, and with each loss, I've learned to observe death not with fear, but with a kind of objectivity. Now, as I face my own mortality, diagnosed with terminal breast cancer at the age of 77, I can't help but wonder: how will my life end?

I recently sat by the bedside of my best friend, who was nearing the end of his life. As he lay there, unable to communicate, I struggled with what to say to someone who might no longer understand me. I had read that in their final stages, people often enter a drowsy state, perhaps transitioning to something beyond our comprehension. Still, I leaned close to his ear and whispered, "Thank you very much for everything you've done for me."

This moment brought into focus the importance of dying with dignity and peace. I am intrigued by hospice services, which provide comfort and support during the final stages of life, allowing for a natural and peaceful death. After my diagnosis, I registered for hospice care, hoping that when the time comes, I can pass away with grace and comfort, surrounded by those who care for me.

As I continue to live with the awareness of my approaching death, I find myself contemplating the essence of life and the inevitable end we all must face. What truly matters is not just how long we live, but how we choose to live and, ultimately, how we choose to say goodbye.

Festivals of Life

If weddings, funerals, and other ceremonies are not the true festivals of life, then what are the moments worth celebrating? I am beginning to approach the final festivals of my life, as I've been living with terminal breast cancer for the past two years. Surprisingly, the treatments have been less grueling than I expected, and, fortunately, I experience little to no pain in my daily life. My days have been relatively peaceful, even allowing me to enjoy simple pleasures like browsing the internet and passing time without the weight of illness pressing too heavily on my mind.

Yet, the disease is relentless, and no one can say how much longer this calm might last. From time to time, anxiety flares up, and I struggle to maintain my focus. In those moments, I find myself philosophizing about life, thinking, "This is just how life is," as if seeking to understand its essence.

This reality has led me to start preparing for the time when I will approach the final stages of life. After consulting with my doctor, who offered no clear answers about my life expectancy, I turned to my own research. Statistically, the life expectancy for someone with terminal breast cancer is around 4-5 years, with a survival rate of about 22%. Having already survived two years, I am aware that, statistically, I may have one to three years remaining. But how do I want to spend this time?

At this stage, there are two things I deeply want to do. One of them is to publish another book. I have a collection of short stories stored on my computer, reflections and insights gathered over the course of my life, including my experiences as a cancer patient. Completing the book may be uncertain, but that doesn't matter. What matters is living each day positively, finding meaning in the time I have left, and filling each day with purpose.

Now, I'm considering the idea of my own "death" as a final celebration of life. Rather than viewing it as an end, I see it as a completion—a festival that marks the end of a long and cherished journey.

Happiness: A Gift for All

Happiness, in its essence, does not discriminate. Whether you are rich or poor, a genius or an ordinary person, the feeling of happiness is uniquely your own. It isn't measured by wealth, status, or intellectual ability, but rather by the lens through which you view your life.

The joy someone feels isn't better or greater than another's—only different, shaped by their perspective and experiences.

I recall a moment of awe when watching a video of a young, brilliant concert violinist performing a complex classical piece. The piece, renowned for its difficulty, was one that only a select few professional players would dare attempt. Captivated, I wondered what drives such mastery. When asked, "When do you feel joy in playing such a challenging piece?" the violinist's response was simple yet profound:

"When I can express the exact sound of the score I envision."

This answer struck me deeply. For most of us, such a feeling of fulfillment might seem out of reach, reserved only for the realm of genius. But happiness is not limited to such extraordinary achievements.

For an ordinary person, joy can be found in everyday moments: the exhilaration of reaching the summit of a mountain after a long climb, the satisfaction of creating a delicious meal, or the simple delight of seeing loved ones enjoy what you've prepared for them.

Our happiness stems from the things that resonate within us personally. What may bring immense joy to one person might not stir the same emotions in another—and that's the beauty of it. Each of us carries the capacity for happiness in our own unique way, shaped by the small, meaningful moments of our daily lives.

This is the wonder of life's big concept of "happiness." It isn't a singular, universal experience but a kaleidoscope of individual joys, each adding color to the tapestry of our shared humanity.

This is the song lyrics which expressed my life in America.

Poem by Fujie Fukuda
Music composed by Kay Shibata
Vocals by Kay Shibata

Beyond SHIOKAZE

I.

Only one word LOVE is on the last page of my diary

The final spark in my heart remains alone

Your smile appears in my mind, then disappears again

There's nothing left, but smeared with ink

Memories that come to my side now, it's the corner of sepia

They say good-bye and are away forever more....

II.

Far from my home land I lived a happy life

Many years have passed, I've missed my loved ones

Looking at the night sky the blinking stars comfort me

My eyes are full of tears, stars fall on my feet

Memories are moving on the ocean wave, they are gone far away

Now I see nothing of my past forever more....

III.

I am thinking of you on Florida Beach alone

Remembering loved ones left behind me

I smile at you but it's illusion in the sky it's gone

Blue sky ocean breeze you are my harmony

Florida is my sweet-heart my life today

And always my life in future, always mine forever more....

(Available on YouTube – 汐風を越えて, "The Last Page of My Diary", Facebook – FUJIE FUKUDA)

Flowers in my backyard

Photo by: J. Grossman

The Sunrise Sky in the Atlantic Ocean

Chapter 4   And........Today in 2024

Throughout my journey of Breast Cancer stage 4, I have been wrote how I had went through in this book which is translated in English from the original was published in Japanese. Now it is in 2024, I am summarized here what I learned from a harsh, sometimes happy memories during these months and years.

Physical Journey and Impact

When I first looked in the mirror after surgery, I barely recognized myself. The familiar parts of my body that had always felt like "me" had transformed, replaced by scars and new textures that felt foreign. My body became a battlefield marked by the memories of surgeries, treatments, and changes. I felt both loss and survival etched into my skin. Over time, I've come to respect and even appreciate these scars. They are my body's way of showing strength, of adapting to survive. I've learned that I am still "me" beneath the changes, but in a way that now includes a history of resilience and fight.

Emotional Journey and Evolution

Emotions have been the stormiest part of this experience. Early on, fear and uncertainty dominated my days. It felt as though I was constantly bracing for impact, living from one appointment to the next. But over time, hope and gratitude found their way in. Today, I feel a quiet resilience that wasn't there before. I've learned to balance worry with optimism, knowing that each new day is something I once feared might not come. Emotions still ebb and flow, but now I embrace them as reminders that I am living and feeling fully again.

Mental and Psychological Growth

This journey fundamentally changed how I see life and myself. I used to worry about things that seem trivial now. My perspective has sharpened; I see the importance of my health and well-being in ways I never truly appreciated before. I used to take time for granted, but now I try to live with purpose, knowing how fragile and precious life is. Cancer gave me the gift of understanding what really matters, and it's brought a new level of mental resilience and inner strength that I didn't know I had.

Identity and Self-Image

My sense of self changed drastically. Before, I was defined by my roles and appearances, things that suddenly felt superficial. I struggled to reconcile my new self-image with the person I used to see in the mirror. Slowly, I started embracing a new identity, one that includes the strength and courage I found along the way. I no longer define myself by outward appearances; my identity is now rooted in a deeper self, one that's been through a storm and come out the other side, transformed but still whole.

Life After Treatment: Challenges and Achievements

One of my proudest moments was simply returning to a normal routine. Small victories, like getting through a day without worry, cooking a meal, or taking a walk, feel monumental now. Life after treatment has its own set of challenges—fear of recurrence lingers, and some days the reminders of what I've been through are strong. But every day that I can move forward, doing the things I love, is a day I count as a victory. I'm proud of finding my way back to the things I love, holding onto life with a fiercer determination.

Spiritual or Existential Reflections

The experience has changed my outlook on life and what it means to be here, to be human. I've developed a newfound respect for life's mysteries and the beauty in small moments. I've also discovered inner sources of strength that I didn't know existed, giving me a deeper understanding of myself and what I believe in. Faith, gratitude, and awe for the world around me have become more meaningful, guiding me through darker days and reminding me of the wonders of simply being alive.

Future Outlook and Hopes

My hopes for the future are now rooted in simplicity—good health, time with loved ones, and a life free of fear. I've learned not to take anything for granted, to celebrate each small milestone. I feel more determined to chase the dreams I once put on hold, embracing the days ahead with a spirit of courage and optimism. I hope to live fully, cherishing the moments I've been given, and creating new memories with those I love.

Message to Others Going Through It

If I could say one thing to others going through this, it's to take things one day at a time. Don't let the fear overwhelm you, even when it seems impossible. Surround yourself with people who lift you up, and know that you're not alone. You're stronger than you realize, and there is life beyond the pain. Embrace each moment, and let yourself feel every emotion—it's all part of the journey. You are resilient, even when you don't feel like it. There's hope, even when the road is dark. And one day, you'll look back and see just how far you've come.

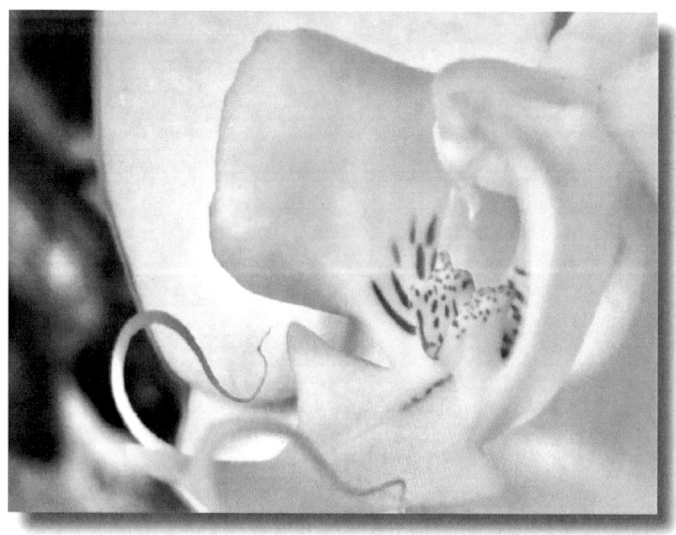

Acknowledgments

Looking back, this journey would not have been possible without the support and guidance of so many remarkable individuals who stood by me.

One of afternoon, as I was resting on the sofa a phone call came in from a familiar number—I'd ignored multiple times. I was consistently declined the offer of publishing my story. But on that day, I picked up. Ms. Ava Lopez from the publishing had guiding and with a way of patiently understanding me. Her kindness and persistence turned my "no" into a grateful "yes," and I appreciate her tremendous efforts for my journey. Including the brilliant publishing team, the editors and designers, thank you for helping bring this book to life.

Special thanks to Mr. James Nakano, my dear friend in London, who undertook the work of translating and refining my words. His careful reviews transformed my pages into something I'm proud to share.

I'd sent him my drafts which were written in poor English, and each time his edits made my words feel polished and truly beautiful.

James, I thank you very much from the bottom of my heart.

Fujie Fukuda

November 2024

Afterword

As I write these words in 2024, we find ourselves living between two worlds: the old, familiar world and the rapidly changing new one. These transformative moments in history, shaping our current era, will one day be studied in classrooms by children of future generations.

Over my 84 years, I have witnessed many historical events that others now read about in history books. I lived through World War II, experienced the shock of President John F. Kennedy's assassination, watched as Americans landed on the moon, and endured the turbulence of economic challenges like the oil crisis. These moments passed not as distant stories but as vivid realities under my own skin.

Today, we face a world shifting in unprecedented ways. The pandemic, for instance, felt like a turning point—a breaking down of old systems and a step toward a world marked by greater uncertainty and upheaval. We see hints of this in the growing dominance of a few over global economies and in the erosion of trust in democratic institutions. Western democracies, once pillars of stability, now face challenges that make us question their strength and direction.

America, too, is changing—gradually yet unmistakably. Whether these changes are good or bad depends on where one stands in the spectrum of political beliefs. For those who cherish traditional, conservative values, this shift may feel like an unwelcome transformation. But such is the nature of history: it moves forward, often driven by the will of the majority, even when it leaves others behind.

In the midst of these societal shifts, I have faced my own battles, particularly with my health. The past several years has tested my resilience, but they have also given me hope—hope for the future, for progress, and for the beauty of what lies ahead, even as I near the close of my own journey.

Reflecting on my life of 84 years, I accept the reality with peace and gratitude. Life, with all its challenges and triumphs, teaches us one unchanging truth: "That is the way it is, and it will be."

About the Author

Fujie Fukuda

Jupiter, Florida, USA
December, 2024

Half a century has passed since I came to America from Japan. At that time, as a young Japanese woman, I could never have dreamed I would one day write a book and publish it in English for an American and Worldwide audience.

Learning a second language—especially English—has been a steep challenge, one I faced later in life as an adult. Yet, thanks to the support and kindness of remarkable friends, I had the privilege of graduating from college and building a life here.

Now, as I approach the later stages of my journey, I feel deeply grateful for the chance to make a small contribution to American society by sharing my story. Writing this book has allowed me to reflect on my experiences, and I hope my words offer insight and encouragement to others. A dear friend once spoke about me in a way that touched my heart, capturing a piece of who I am. Though he is no longer with us, I hold his words close and imagine him smiling down from heaven, proud of what I've achieved.

"Our Fujie"

Like the waves of the ocean

In perpetual motion,

At the edge of the sea,

Calm in reflection,

Sensitive to perfection

In art and harmony......

~By Bertram Spector

In Memory of...

Every year, toward the end of January, the coldest weather reaches South Florida. An arctic blast sweeps down the North American continent, and suddenly our warm peninsula shares in the chill that grips the northern states.

January 20, 2025, was Inauguration Day for the American president. Like most Americans, I celebrated with hope for a brighter future—even if my own future felt uncertain.

During this hopeful time, my beloved cat, Kelly, had been very sick for about a week. I watched him closely, noticing how he ate less each day. Eventually, he stopped eating altogether, and I knew the time had come to say goodbye.

On January 22, 2025, I faced the heartbreaking decision to part with Kelly after 16 wonderful years of companionship. It was a cold, rainy day, and my home felt unbearably quiet. Friends and family offered comforting words and messages, but my grief was overwhelming.

I understand that this is nature's way for all living creatures. Still, adjusting to life without Kelly has been difficult. It's been five days since I've been alone in my empty house, and only now can I write about him without tears.

I've put away his belongings in hopes of easing my sadness and returning to a semblance of normalcy. The memories of our time together remain a blessing, and though I miss him dearly, I know this is for the best, especially given my own health and age.

Fortunately, my book, KAENJU, was still in progress, allowing me the chance to honor Kelly's memory here. I will always cherish the love and comfort he brought into my life.

www.ingramcontent.com/pod-product-compliance
Lightning Source LLC
Chambersburg PA
CBRC090824120626
46547CB00007B/601